Wolves

Beverley Randell

Contents

Wolves and dogs

Wolves look like large dogs.

Wolf

Huskies and German Shepherds are dogs that look very like wolves, but they are smaller.

Husky

German Shepherd

All dogs are descended from wolves, and that is why they look like them. If wolves breed with dogs, their puppies are big and strong.

Wolves and dogs behave in similar ways: they have an excellent sense of smell; they scavenge for scraps; they eat meat; they bark and growl. Wolves are often playful and friendly with each other, but, just like dogs, they can be fierce.

Wolves and dogs are tireless runners. They chase other animals. They wag their tails when they are glad, and tuck them down between their legs when they are scared.

When do wolves tuck their tails down between their legs?

Wolves live in family packs

Most wolves live together in families with about six or seven adult wolves. The leader of the pack is the strongest male. He is the father of all the cubs in the pack. He is the only wolf who has a mate.

The pack leader holds his tail high in the air to show that he is the boss. The other wolves keep their tails down. Sometimes the wolves lie on their backs to make it clear that they will not fight the leader.

Wolves tuck their tails down between their legs when they are scared.

Each wolf knows its place in the pack. One wolf is the underdog that everyone snarls at. All the wolves nuzzle the leader, to show him they will obey him. He decides when it is time to hunt and where the pack will go.

How does a wolf show that it does not want to fight?

Wolf pups and growing cubs

Three to twelve wolf pups are born in underground dens in early spring. Dens are often dug under tree roots in sandy banks.

At first, the mother wolf stays with her pups in the warm, dry den. She licks them, and suckles them. She cannot go hunting, so other wolves in the pack bring her food. When the pups are three weeks old, they come out of the den to play and to fight. Now they can stand on their back legs to suckle.

By lying on its back, a wolf shows that it does not want to fight.

The pups fight each other to decide who is the strongest.

When the cubs are two months old, they move to a sheltered meadow with the rest of the pack.

Their new home must be near water because wolves drink a lot. When the pack hunts for food, an adult wolf stays behind to guard the cubs from bears and eagles.

Where are wolf cubs born?

Hunting in spring and summer

All wolves chase and eat anything that moves, even worms, grasshoppers, lizards, mice and frogs. The young cubs practise pouncing on these small creatures.

In the summer, full-grown wolves chase rabbits, hares, ducks and ground squirrels. They eat eggs. They catch fish in streams and rivers.

When wolves get wet, they shake themselves dry, just as dogs do.

Wolf cubs are born in underground dens.

When a wolf returns from hunting, the cubs leap up and lick its face. The wolf brings up lumps of the fresh meat that it has just eaten, and the cubs gulp it down.

All the wolves in the pack help feed the cubs until they are seven months old. Then they are big enough to keep up with their family on the hunting trail.

Who feeds the wolf cubs?

Hunting in autumn and winter

Many small creatures hibernate in winter, so wolves have to hunt larger animals. If the wolves kill a caribou there is enough meat for the whole pack. Extra meat can be buried and eaten later.

But hunting big animals is not easy. Caribou run fast and most can escape. When wolves find a herd of caribou, they try to make the animals run. If an animal is old or slow, the wolves attack it together. Sometimes they chase a frightened animal for hours before they manage to leap on it, and kill it.

All the wolves in the pack help feed the cubs.

Musk oxen and moose will turn and charge the wolves, and kick out with their large hoofs. Their kicks can crack bones. Wolves are wary, but they sometimes get hurt.

Wolves chasing musk oxen

Why do wolves sometimes bury meat?

Wolves communicate

Wolves in a pack seem to know what the other wolves are planning to do. Then they act together. In deep snow, wolves take turns to run in front and break a trail for the others to follow.

They bury meat to eat later.

Just like dogs, wolves use their tails and ears, and sometimes their whole bodies, to show their feelings. They show anger by curling back their lips and snarling.

Wolves whine and growl, bark and howl. Every sound means something different.

How do wolves show anger?

Wolves howl

Before wolves set out for a night's hunting, they stand together, lift their noses, and howl loudly. The eerie noise travels a long way. The howl of one pack of wolves is often answered by the howl of another.

The howls may warn other packs to keep their distance.

Wolves show anger by curling back their lips and snarling.

Sometimes a wolf will howl if it gets separated from its pack. When the pack howls in reply, the wolf knows where to find its family.

When do packs of wolves howl?

Where wolves live

People fear wolves because they attack sheep and cattle. For thousands of years, farmers have killed wolves. The few wolves that are left are found far away in the mountains, or in the frozen north.

The Arctic (North Pole)

wolves

The Antarctic (South Pole)

Packs of wolves often howl at night, before they go out hunting.